POEMS OF LOVE
AND AWAKENING

John Welwood

ISBN-13:978-1502780157

ISBN-10:1502780151

The first edition of this book was published in 2004. This second edition contains nine new poems, along with minor edits of the others. Three poems from the first edition have been removed.

Special acknowledgment and thanks to Tai Sheridan for his invaluable help in publishing this volume.

Table of Contents

Foreword

The poems in this book have been written over the past fifty years, and it has been a joy to bring them together and publish them in this volume. The two main themes of the poems— love and awakening—are also the main themes of my work and life journey as a whole. Most of the love poems were written to my wife and consort of thirty years, Jennifer, while others were written to loves during the earlier years of my life.

While few of these poems need any explanation, several may benefit from a brief commentary. Two poems—*Everything Co-emerges* and *Co-emergence*—draw on the notion of co-emergence, a Buddhist term I am using to signify how our ordinary humanity and our ultimate, spiritual nature always arise together inseparably, as two interwoven dimensions of our experience. The feeling of this boundary and overlap between the human and the spiritual holds a special magic for me. It is what has often inspired the words of a poem to take birth.

Thus the spirit of co-emergence permeates many of the poems in this book. *Becoming Human* is another example. It was written during a workshop I was teaching, in which I was intrigued with the ordinary, beautifully idiosyncratic human qualities of the people in the group, a few of whom I mention at the beginning. In this poem I wanted to honor the lovely mystery of the human person, and offset the tendency in some spiritual circles to focus on pure transcendence at the expense of human embodiment.

> *Some say we're humans becoming buddhas,*
> *But I'd say we're buddhas waking up in human form.*

John Welwood
October, 2014

Poems of Love

You are My Star

You are my star, my light,
I am your druid in the night.
Our hearts are bound together,
No matter what we say or do.
Let us awaken together, love.

I'm Glad You Came

You came here
Sliding down a beam of light,
Reluctantly at first,
Not knowing if you wanted to belong
To this school where suffering is path.
I'm glad you came.
For on those long dark nights
When I lie awake and wonder
What it's all about,
And where humanity went wrong,
I think of you,
And know the universe is friendly after all.

The Open Space of You

I lie at rest
In the open space
Of your being
As in a sea of shining grass,
On soft green days in early spring.

There is this lightness
At your core
That lets me know
That I am home,
Our souls enfolded ever so gently
In the arc of each other's embrace.

Let everything between us then
Compose itself around this open space
In which we lie together,
Like dreamers in a field of light.

Jenny

I come to you
As though called to worship.
The light in your hands
Enters my dark corners,
Opening all my knots and folds.
You teach through the lightness you ride on.
And still, after all these years,
I long to know:
Where is the source of your joy?

Everything Co-emerges

Everything co-emerges with emptiness—
My love for you,
Your golden hair,
The look on your face when we said goodbye,
The flight to London on an empty plane,
Thoughts of loving-kindness,
My longing for the rain,
Our hearts melting together,
The pain of being two.

Everything co-emerges with emptiness,
Even my love for you.

Protecting You

For so long have we been swimming
In the ocean of our love,
That this water has become translucent space,
The almost invisible ground that holds up all our days.

But now, as death comes near,
My love for you transforms into a spear in my hands,
Sharpened for battle,
A line cast deep into your heart,
Holding you to me,
A focused beam of light
In which your luminous beauty stands revealed,
More brightly than ever before.

Rain of Blessings

You've showered me with love,
Now it's time to let love hold *you*
Fast in its embrace.

You've given others strength:
Now may you know it as your own,
The ever-present ground.

You've brought light to this world,
Let this light now heal you from within.

May all that you have given
Return now as a rain of blessings
Washing through your every cell,
So you may know that you are loved at last.

Held from deep within,
May you rest like a babe at ease
In life's kind and welcoming arms.

Blood on My Paws

I came to you with blood on my paws.
And you saw the wild wolf in my heart,
Who nuzzled up beside the beauty of your soul.
You were my passage to new life,
I softened in your golden grace.

We shared a vision of love,
Of how it breathes the fire of transformation
Into this earthly clay,
To forge a heart that's crystal clear.

Yet as a vine, once pruned, grows back more thickly,
So, as years went by,
The shadows of our past crept back upon us.
I took your love for granted,
And you endured my forgetfulness,
While the rage built up inside you.

Forgive me now for all that I have missed,
For all the ways I fell asleep,
Failing to honor the gift you are to me.

Forgive me please,
It was never you I meant to hurt,
I came to you with bloody paws.
I was only fending off ghosts,
Not you, my golden beauty.

Now as I lie broken, bleeding,
I can only pray:
May it bear fruit, this devastation,
May it tear down the walls of separation,
And may the new life rising from within
Serve everyone and all.

Only You

Only you
Can undo me,
The intense heat of your wrath
Breaking me open from within.
I want to fall into your fire,
To melt and be reborn,
That I may serve you,
Hold you,
And love you
With a heart wide open.
Only you
Have given me
This precious jewel.

Loving You Reveals to Me

Loving you,
I taste the fullness of my heart.
Touching this fullness,
I know the joy of life.
Receiving this joy,
I find a home within my body.
Settling deep within this,
I'm who I'm meant to be.

Oh what a wonder:
Loving you reveals to me
The one I've always been.

I've Seen Your Fire

I've seen your fire
I've seen your light
I've seen your lion roaring in the night.

I've known you tender
I've known you strong
I've known your soul and heard its song.

I've felt you near
I've felt you far
All told, I love you— as you are.

Turning Fifty

You're lovely, you're tender,
You're beautiful, you're wise.
And I knew that the first time
I looked into your eyes.

Your smile is a-glowing,
Your warmth, it overflows,
Your heart, a green meadow,
Your mind, it always knows.

Fifty years have gone by now,
You're still a shining star,
And I love you, I cherish you
For all the things you are.

Song on her Breasts

Your breasts are like the ocean—
I swim in their fathomless space.
They rise like ancient continents,
Their primordial magic sizzling on my tongue.
They comfort me on long, dark nights,
Telling me of other worlds, other lifetimes,
Lost to us now,
Yet here for the tasting
In this long, soft kiss.

Repertoire

the pain of loving
the pain of not loving
the pain of trying to love
the pain of trying not to love
the pain of pretending to love
the pain of pretending not to love
the pain of showing love
the pain of not showing love
the pain of reaching out
the pain of pulling back
the pain of loving

Entering You

I want to enter you and peel off your skin
From inside; to explode you gently,
With the stroking of hands,
To uncover the quivering light within,
And tell you there's no need to hide,
Nor cause for anything but joy.

Inside You

Like being at the top of space,
Inside you,
Open and alert on all four sides,
Let's not make a big deal
Out of this.

Tender One

Stars falling from the heavens
Land at your feet.
I see you walking among them,
And wonder how your tender spirit
Survives this world,
From what source you flow,
Feeding my streams
That run all night long
Steadily homeward,
Only lingering in pools
To reflect your stars.

Silence after Loving

Now in swiftly descending darkness I rise,
Borne on a swell of love undeclared.
I go to the window,
And watch the crowds weave dumbly home.
You come sit beside me,
And gently watch the sky grow night.

Summer Absence

You are gone now,
The breezes of your absence
Swirling round me
On this summer's afternoon.
Yet your presence is with me still,
Mingling with trees, ocean, and the sky.

Who is this you I want?
You is just a name-tag
For greater being, which lies all around,
And inside too.

Warrior of Love

You're sitting in your room,
You're gazing into space,
You're far away from me
You're still inside my heart.

We're walking on the path,
We're dancing on the edge,
So much energy between us,
So much love that wants to flow.

I want to make a child,
You want to roam the wild.
The warrior of love
Dances on the edge of contradiction.

So let us dance,
And smile, and cry.
The dignity of sadness
Is the fullness of the heart.

Your Gift

In rain or sunlight,
In pain or delight,
At all times
And all ways,
You are a gift in my life.

Your Buns

You slipped into my life
Under cover of night,
And installed yourself there
With your flashing blue eyes
And your sassy buns wiggling shamelessly.

Will There Ever Be

Will there ever be another little clown,
To come along and turn me upside-down,
To ransack all my cupboards and my drawers,
Seeking out the clues to who I was,
To pore through my love letters on the sly,
And endless ask about old lives gone by,
Like you did,

            Once,

                    Long ago?

Basic Goodness

When I think of you
 And our time together,
 Smiles rise up inside me.
 Display of basic goodness—
 How good to share it
 In this troubled world,
 Even for a while.

Three-Line Poems

Full and crazy like the moon,
Raw like the wind off the sea,
Wild like the love I feel for you: this living heart.
***

The rain on the roof is like our life,
Falling like tears from my cheeks.
Falling, falling, endlessly falling.
***

Pain seeks to constrict my heart.
So I feed it all my love—
Feed it apples and oranges and gray rainy days.
***

Anger flaming white
Burns through attachment,
Ashes and silence scatter on the wind.
***

My heart is as wide as the sea,
I don't know how far it reaches.
If it touches you, will you let me know?
***

Walking in moonlight on the beach,
Your spirit rustling through my hair,
I reach up and kiss the night.

Words for the Wind

I see your soul in everything,
Lady of the radiant heart.
In you all things are flowing,
Your light a spectacle of grace,
Wakening my third eye to what's beyond seeing,
Sending me reeling with drunken bliss
Of a wild heart brimming over.

How can there be such a one as you?
My desire dissolves when I taste your beauty,
And I am aligned in your presence.
You open me to landscapes of the soul
Once glimpsed, and long forgotten.

Sometimes in the the mornings
I catch myself wanting you,
But I know that you move in your own time,
That is one
With all the silent things of the world.

Loving and Letting Go

I.

I want you to soar
High like a hawk
Circling in the pregnant sky.
What wants to give birth?
I want you to be free and strong,
Like a lion roaming high mountain plains.
I want to love you more than myself.
What wants to give birth?
It feels immense.
Shivering in the wind,
I turn home to wait out the storm.

II.

Drops of rain splatter on dry earth,
Kicking up little clouds of dust,
Like someone who cannot accept
A gift that she's not ready for.
My love washes down the canyons,
Collecting in little pools that reflect the sun,
Riding the rapids of the heart,
Growing stronger at each turn.
Unstoppable now, I have to let it go.
Too strong to contain,
Too deep to fathom,
Too wide to be known,
Too good to be true:
Still, all my streams run to you.

Tristesse

Thousands of times I have sung to you
In your absence.
These days are but the petals of a rose
That fall and wither up.

Forever Burning

I love you as the days and years keep turning,
And I come to know you less and more,
My love for you forever brightly burning,
Deep within my ancient, shining core.

Mother

You were my teacher first and last.

You held me in your arms and gave without reserve.

You lent me your fear and darkness too,

To wear as a cloak as I pass through this world.

As a girl, you radiated light and joy,

As a woman, life began to disappoint you.

When you brought me into this world,

You were already losing the battle with your pain.

I always wanted to save you,

But I never could.

I could only turn away to find my life.

One day I returned to find you entirely vulnerable,
You the child, me the parent.
I wanted to take you in my arms
And make everything right,
Feeling all your kindness
And the tenderness I'd turned away from,
Grateful at last for all that you had done for me.

On my way to tell you this,
You chose to leave this world, in a flash.
And I found my heart once more, broken in pieces,
Wishing I could start all over .

Now in the end, your soul is set loose
From all the darkness you inherited here,
Go free, dear one,
May you rest at last in the arms of love.

Dangerous Beauty

Women of power,
You stood against the mighty onslaught of the judges,
The Inquisitor's harsh hand bore down on you,
Seeking to crush the life within your bones,
The life that they had long ago foresworn.

Women of power,
Your time is coming.
The time to loose the fire of creation,
You've had so long to hide below the ground.
Soon, soon the hour is approaching
When you can let it burn with full abandon,
No longer having to protect
All those who would be threatened by your blaze.

Women of power,
I now invite you
To step into this world that needs you so,
To put aside the silence that has served you,
And voice all you have known but never said.

Women of power,
The earth is crying,
And you alone
Can bear her in your arms.

Long Life Supplication

For Jennifer

Your heart, the essence of kindness,
Your mind, the essence of truth,
Your spirit, a light that dispels darkness,
Your soul, an abode of sweetness and love,
You who walk on a carpet of grace
Through this tangled world,
You who care for all creatures
And see the beauty in the heart of the beast,
You whose joy spreads across the green hills
And rustles through the forests,
May you remain here a long time,
May you be healthy in body and soul,
May you live to flower in fruition.
I supplicate all benevolent angels and protectors

To guard your life and health,
To lend you strength where you need it,
And to help you stay here
With every one of us who loves you
And is blessed by your tender presence.

Your Eyes

When I look into your eyes, into your eyes,
What is it I see, what do I see?
I see the mysteries,
The mysteries are what I see...
And the clear steady gaze of truth.

Goodness Unceasing

You are the morning clothed in golden light,
I am the rustling silence of the night.
Goodness unceasing rains down on all who see,
Sweetness increasing as I gaze on thee....

Poems of Awakening

Forget about Enlightenment

Forget about enlightenment.

Sit down wherever you are

And listen to the wind singing in your veins.

Feel the love, the longing, the fear in your bones.

Open your heart to who you are, right now,

Not who you'd like to be,

Not the saint you're striving to become,

But the being right here before you, inside you, around you.

All of you is holy.

You're already more and less

Than whatever you can know.

Breathe out,

Touch in,

Let go.

Vulnerable

Always be vulnerable
To your pain, your fear, your loneliness,
To your pleasure too, and your joy,
To all that travels through you.
Don't close the doors
To these pilgrims from a far-off land,
But welcome them all—
One a wild, restless spirit
Secretly longing to be tamed,
Another a lover on a long, sweet night,
Who only wants to melt in your embrace.
For this is how you grow—
By including everything.

Always, always be vulnerable
To all that you are.

Becoming Human

Avram brings the New York Times each day
And leaves it on the floor unread,
Tackling the crossword puzzle instead.
Noland is working on a house in Thailand,
While Rob works on his understanding.
Rosamond watches Cassandra's every move,
And Michele keeps on wondering about it all.

Each of us leaves a trail of clues
To the mystery whose life we live.
Some say we're humans becoming buddhas,
But I'd say we're buddhas waking up in human form.
Each look, each step, and every tender glance
Stands on its own,
Fleeting glimpses of the formless taking form,
Before the good, gentle space gathers them back again.

Wherever You Are

Wordless sounds swarming in the night,
Radiance of silence rustling all around,
What is left when all is left behind?
Rest in that, wherever you are,
Now,
And now again.

First Moment

First moment,
Holy moment,
Where no one can abide—
It is quite clear
It's only here
That all is well.

Satsang

Versions from Poonjaji

I.

Throw away your oars.

Break the mast!

Let your boat be pulled into the whirlpool.

Then keep quiet

And the rest will take care of itself.

II.

Everything rises and falls,

Yet you remain untouched.

When you look within,

You see that all of this

Is a rainbow painted in space.

Where is sorrow

When all the cosmos rises and falls in you?

III.

I is the same in everyone,

Though the bodies are different.

How have you, the changeless,

Come to identify with that which changes?

How much time does it take to go home

When you're already sitting at home?

IV.

First you disappear.

Then you dive into the ocean of ambrosia.

Then whatever you speak will be poetry.

Then there is no one speaking.

(Composed using phrases, with a few small alterations, from the satsangs, or spiritual dialogues, of the late Indian master, Sri H. W. Poonja.)

Great Perfection

You bring the world alive each moment,
In the freshness of your look,
Your touch, your waking.
Recognize this, your creation, at last.
It is always arising anew,
In each moment of looking freshly,
Letting everything happen as it does,
Without making something out of it.

You thought you were cold and hungry,
Wandering lost in an alien place,
But now you can see:
This world is your light show,
Everything shining and shimmering,
In the blaze of your presence.
Be glad then.
Go forth nakedly
And claim your royal seat.

Great Dharmakaya

My whole mind and body
All aglow
In vast, illumined space,
Which holds me
In its tenderest embrace.

What is this love, I ask,
How can it be?
That everything
And nothing
Is in love with me?

Subtle Body

Letting down
Into the feeling body,
I offer myself
To the welcoming earth.
And settling now
Into this flowing body,
I melt into
Streams of drizzling bliss.

Why bother holding up
When letting down is such a joy?
If up is where I need to be
Then let this spine be raised toward heaven,
Yes, and let the sky pour down my veins.

Cascade Canyon Prayers

I.
Like a cascade pouring
Into the rocky pool below,
May your grace stream through me.
I have come to the end of my search.
I no longer know what I'm looking for.
When I turn inside, all I find
Is the tension of holding on
To something— anything
Just to prove that I exist.
Now let your torrent flow through me,
That I may give up
And come down,
To wash up like a leaf
On your holy shore.

II.
The singing of this brook
Reminds me of the music
I have locked inside my bones.
Long ago I turned away
And went into the jungle of the world
In search of glory.
But now I have come back.
I can think of nothing better
Than to sit here beside you,
And listen to your song,
And let it stir my longing
For what... I cannot name.

III.
Joy of water flowing
Delighted in your knowing
That nothing can prevent you
From going home.

I'd love to stay beside you,
But soon I must be going,
I cannot keep from sowing
Seeds of what's to come.

But would you flow inside me?
May you always guide me
And lead me to the stream
That is my own.

Change of Life

This morning I wake up
Knowing without a doubt
That I must change my life
In every way,
From inside out.

I have not loved enough.

What would it be like,
To let my heart
Open fully to this aching world?

And what else is there to do?

New Birth

I want to be born,

To step out of darkness

And reach out my hand.

I want to feel space all around

And touch each moment as the first and last.

I want to break through the shell of sleep,

And let all my senses breathe.

I want to rise from the belly,

And shine love all around,

I want to give birth.

Prayer

Something in me wants to speak,
I know not what it is.
A question at the bottom of the heart
Is rising to my lips:
What is a life?
What makes it unassailable?
Am I just to do what I do
With all of myself?
Or is there another, hidden call
Beyond all doing?
Must I wander off to India
To find the secret spice
That will make all my days taste rich?
Can I not read the hieroglyphic of my life
Right here, in the movement of the clouds

This listless morning,
In the presence of this hour
That harbors all that is to come?

I do not want to move,
I don't want any plans.
I want to be lifted
By some unknown force inside me
And carried in its arms.
I want the way to stand clear before me,
I want to follow, not lead,
I want to open all my senses,
So I can heed the call.

Now I can feel what's rising in me,
And offer the only prayer that there is:
Carry me now,
Let me follow your way.

Celebrating the Black

Celebrate the blackness.
You first thought it was nothing
But descent into darkness, never to return.
You fled the empty places,
The falling away of familiar hopes and plans
That held you together.
You turned it into depression,
Thinking there was something wrong with you
That you couldn't keep it together,
That you were full of holes,
That you were but a feather
In the winds blowing through you.
You imagined you were the only one
Like this, so slight and insubstantial.

But the truth is so much kinder:
You see, we're all spun out of this blackness —
Bliss of silence, glow of emptiness.
We all contain dark caverns inside us,

Where nothing is happening
Save the brilliance of clarity, the mystery of space.
We're all floating in the dark satin expanse
Of pure being, illumined from within.

Out of this blackness
Indestructible peacefulness flows, endlessly,
With nothing to interrupt it forever.
It is the peace of death, and even more,
The stillness at the heart of the living.
All of us are seeking this, constantly,
Even when we hate ourselves for all we've left undone.
All our wars have been fought
For this peace at the core
That dissolves all opposition
And lets us rest at last in the arms of grace
That enfold us, always.

Look now into the deep night sky
And know that this blackness pervades you,
And welcomes you back
To the only home that is your own.

Storm on Lago d'Orta

Here on this lake
Where Nietzsche found and lost
The only woman he could ever hope to love,
The storm rains down relentlessly for days on end,
Forcing me to sit indoors,
Contemplating the waters
And island chapel of San Giulio,
With forty monks praying at its core,
Surrounded by a merciless parade
Of Italian tourists— pensioners out for the afternoon,
Hauled in by the busload, day after day.
They burst into the basilica
Where the saint lies in state,
Filling the vaulted aisles
With clucks and squawks,
Like a flock of hungry geese being fed.

No use to ask why they've come here,
No use to contemplate the forces
That create these busloads of empty faces
Desperately trying to fill up their days
By trampling on the holy silence.

No use to protest that whatever
Retains its slender beauty in this wasted world
Only draws these hordes of hungry souls
To gawk, take photos, fill an empty day, and be gone,
Gradually sucking out the last remains of the holy
Still residing in the ancient stones.

It's happening everywhere:
Beauty cut down, holiness despoiled.
Am I one of the despoilers too?
What is the shard of the sacred I look for here?
I seek an ancient thread of wisdom
Now long fled from the outer world,
A jewel no pilgrimage can deliver,
So close it's hard to find.
I too trample on it like the tourists in the temple
And banish it with idle talk.

The storm is saying it's time to move on
I listen, thanking the rain,
And turn home to the silence within.

What a Way to Spend the Days

For Kobun

Everything's gone to black-and-white
This third day of sesshin.
I want to go home
And rest my head,
Churning with thoughts
Bursting out all over,
And the never-ending question:
Why am I always dying?

But you just laugh.
You're not much help, you know.
Just sitting there,
Your face broken through with smiles
Like the spring fields gone to grasses.
You're nothing more than being here, with us

Which makes me less alone,
Though no less lonely,
And somehow feeling better
Though nothing hurts the less.

The days pass on,
It's all the same,
Sometimes a glimpse—
It has no name.

Inside and Out

This morning you want to curl up
And retreat from the world.
All right then, give in to your desire,
And let yourself come to rest within.
Welcome yourself home.
There's nothing you must do,
And nothing you must say.
Only stillness, inhabiting silence.

Soon there is a stirring,
Something bubbling up from below:
A natural urge to reach out,
Only this time shining forth
Your radiance from within.

Bedford Springs

If love is full of holes,
What is it we see in each other?
Just when you think you've got it,
Everything slips away.
Vajrayana shatters reality
So that we can learn to be kind.

Lying awake at night,
Listening to space
And crackling with vajra fever,
Resistance breaks out like sweat,
Passion flows like blood,
And surrender follows like tears—
Offerings to the guru:
Teach me to dance in your fire.

And Now You Are Dead

For Chogyam Trungpa

And now you are dead,
After all.
Yet your mind keeps unfolding,
And your vast heart keeps beating
Inside me.
I don't know whether to laugh or to cry ,
But then with you, I never did.

You saw what was needed
And had to be done.
You took up a sword.
You chewed up this world,
And swallowed it whole.
I guess that killed you in the end,
As everything does,
But not before it made you blaze.

You cared so much,
You couldn't care less.
Yet you went right on
Tickling our minds,
Breaking open our hearts,
Spilling our blood on your sword.

I owe you everything.
You showed me my mind
And asked me to dance.
Your death was the final blessing:
It let me know how much I love you.

Gratefully Yours

Just to have eyes,
That I may see the colors
Of your luminous presence everywhere,
For this alone, I give thanks.

Just to have ears,
That I may hear the music
Of your sonorous silence,
For this alone, I am grateful.

Just to have speech,
That I may give voice
To all the subtle shadings
Of how it is to be here,
For this alone, I offer praise.

Just to inhabit this human body,
That I may know you in my blood and bones,
For this alone, I am your servant.

Just to be here,
Just for this time,
However long it lasts,
For this alone, I bow down.

Having Myself

Joy in my heart
To have myself at last.
This, just this
Is what I've always wanted,
Is what I've always sought.
Everything is here
In this fullness of presence.

The night welcomes and holds me,
There is nowhere else to go.

Yang

Renounce the gentle arts,
Take up a stick and beat the ground,
Whirl in a storm of screaming heat,
Run at the winds that beat you back,
And swim, swim for all you're worth,
Up the current of the never-ending light.

Aloneness

Feeling the beauty of the world,
You always want to share it with someone.
Listen:
Rest softly in it,
Don't say anything about it
To anyone,
Not even to yourself.

Perfect Moment

Mist breaking up across the face of Mt. Tam.
For a moment she coyly bares her shoulders,
Before hiding again behind her flowing robe.

On the window before me,
A spider balances on a silken thread.
Through the filaments of its web
I watch the play of cloud and mountain.

In the background, Schubert's piano impromptus
Fill the space with yearning.
In the midst of all this, I start my new book.

Mountain, mist, spider, Schubert, soul unfolding in words:
The play of life around me, in me, as me.
Some would say: "different expressions of God."
I say nothing, but only enter in.

The Kiss

Don't throw yourself away.
Or hide away inside.
Inside and outside meet, touch, and kiss
Only through you.
And in this kiss you come alive.
All else is grasping and rejecting.

Being is a breeze that blows through you.
To ripple in this breeze is bliss.

Full Lake

It all comes down to this:
Full lake, empty of intent,
Fish leaping from water,
Ripples spreading out.
Let the fish leap.
Enjoy the display.
If you try to catch one,
You'll only get caught in your nets.

Where is your Mind?

Where is your mind when you listen to the rain?
What is your thought but a ripple on the wind?
Magic happens at the edge of thunder and silence.
So brilliant and profound: This simple human presence.
Nothing can arise unless you let it fall.

Look Without a Looker

Look without a looker,
See without a sight,
Then rest,
Hanging still for a moment,
Gliding through space
Without a place to land.

Then, without saying a word,
Show me who you are.

Mandala

You open the gate
Through your willingness to meet yourself.
To meet yourself is to go to the edge,
To teeter on the verge of the abyss
And let go—
To fall, flailing at first,
Regretting, or looking for someone to blame.
But as you keep falling,
You learn to stretch out,
To rest in the space that enfolds you.
You discover that it welcomes you,
Holds you, and cares for you.
It only wants you to unfold
And arise as who you really are.

Look now, you've entered in:
The mandala of self-existing wisdom.

Co-emergence

You break at last into laughter,
Headache follows soon thereafter.
Sweat on palms goes dry,
Turning into tears you cry.
Is this pain or is it gladness?
I cannot separate joy and sadness.
Dark night or day light—
Ah, the open sky.

To Contact the Author

John Welwood
PO Box 2173
Mill Valley, CA 94942

You can purchase this book
in print or as an eBook
at amazon.com

44145126R00059

Made in the USA
Middletown, DE
29 May 2017